LETTERS ON STEROIDS: Confessions of an addicted Letter-To-The-Editor writer

By

Jim Green

Dedicated To:

All who want to make the world a better
place--

PROLOGUE

Best guess is that I have written over
5,000 Letters To The Editor, over the
years—some I never mailed [in the past
15 years emailed]—many were never
printed—Most dealt with a Washington
that is deaf as an adder regarding
mainstream America—

Compulsive letter writers, incidentally,
do not go looking for a computer/word-
processor—they look up and one
magically appears before them—and
more often than not they have no idea

how they got there [only a slight exaggeration]—

The letters are self-explanatory—topical to events at the time—and unfailing in a Democrat slant—I can't imagine why anyone in their right mind would vote Republican—

The "Goldwater Republicans" made a little more sense—after all, Goldwater supported gays in the military and a woman's right to choose—and like every rational person, today, the "social conservatives" gave Goldwater the heebee jeebees—

But the celebration of Reagan—like he was a great president—is mind-shattering—he was a horrible president!

And history will record that he was the worst president in American history, until Bush II came along and bumped him out of last place—

Also the history revisionists propaganda—and hypocrites like Gingrich—and those who thought Reagan should be given a state funeral [an event as phony as the crocodile tears shed at Kim Jong-il's funeral]—is nauseating--

Many seem to have forgotten that our deficit was a very manageable $60 billion in 1980—through mismanagement, fraud, pandering to the greed of their wealthiest contributors, etc.,—Reaganomics had escalated our deficit to a staggering $10 trillion by 2008—

And it has taken an additional $4 trillion to mop up the mess caused by this corrupt Republican agenda! Bush I, hit the nail on the head when he called it "VooDoo Economics"!

So where is the Republican apology?

During the Republican primary in 2012—and absent a profuse apology to the American people for the damage Reaganomics did to America—every candidate, including Romney, stated that they intend to pick up where Bush II left off—if elected!

Do they think we Americans are idiots------? Don't answer that--

For clarity, we need to define Reaganomics: Siphon America's wealth out of the hands of the consuming middle—give it to the 1%--[and the big lie is] they will build factories with the windfall of cash—everyone will then

have a job in the corporation—and we
will all live happily ever after—

Yes folks, it is a fairy tale—but a fairy
tale with a nightmare ending! For one,
siphoning America's wealth away from
the consuming middle has a shelf-life of
about 7 years before it sends the
economy into meltdown—as it did in
1987 & 2008—

And in both cases it took a ton of cash
from the taxpayers [driving our deficit
into a deeper and deeper hole] to put a
floor under an economy in meltdown—

And while we should be putting on the tombstone for Reaganomics: IT DOESN'T WORK! It is inexplicably alive and well---with Romney promising, if elected, even deeper tax cuts for the 1%--It is the Republican One and Only Program!

Again, do they think we Americans are idiots? Again, don't answer that----

In large part, our nemesis [and may well do us in] is a paralysis with fear from the hysteria of McCarthyism—with the Republican propaganda machine working day and night to exploit—to frighten our "frightened ones"—

Yes, we have a Commie behind every tree and they are going to jump out and get us—BOO! This whole devious scheme by the Republican Party is despicable, nauseating--as well as patently absurd!

Despicable, because their sole objective in exploiting our "frightened ones"—is so that while they are distracted with this nonsense—the Republican Party can carry out its One and Only program--to pander to the GREED of their wealthiest contributors!

A final note to the reader, the letters are not in sequence [the unemployment rate is relevant to the time written], and about letter writing. Each letter is intended to be comprehensive in itself— i.e., the objective is to give a different slant [to add clarity] to a subject that may be static—for instance "Reaganomics"—thus, please look past the zingers, i.e., redundancy and look for the nuggets—Thx!

Chapter One [of One]: Politics 2012, etc.

To the editor:

"Conservative" is the big word in Republican parlance in this election— and the candidates stumble all over themselves to say it as many times possible is their 30 second ads--

Indeed, Romney referred to himself as "severely conservative" and even declared that he was "more conservative than Rick Santorum" [which is way out there]—and he went on to say "I'm not concerned about the very poor".

But in drilling down on this a bit—the Republican candidates are obviously trying to appeal to persons who embrace being "conservative"—but what does this mean?

There are different ways to be conservative—a person can be fiscally conservative, and be socially "liberal", or vice-versa—but you get the sense that "severely conservative" is code for I'm not a "liberal".

And after years of Republicans demonizing the word "liberal" in their propaganda ads--it is little wonder that in their prayers at night their followers thank God they are not a "liberal"—

But those who define themselves as "conservative" might do well to look up the definition of the antonym for the word "liberal"--"illiberal" in Webster's.

And the real shocker for those who are slaves to the labels, i.e., propaganda buzz words, in this election will be shocked to learn that if they buy car insurance—they are a "socialist"—

Yep folks, our car insurance is based on the same collectivist principle as "socialism"—we pool our money to protect us when fate taps us on the shoulder—

And communism differs only in that it is controlled by a totalitarian state dominated by a single and self-perpetuating political party, which, of course, is also its fatal flaw.

Indeed, it is this flaw that has made the extremes on both the right and the left—fascism and communism, fail. It takes a dictator to hold the government in place in both cases—and it is the antithesis of a democracy.

In sum, what we need is a "post-label" election—to cut out the noise so the electorate will actually listen what the candidates are saying.

For instance, when Romney says that he wants to cut taxes for the 1% ever further it is consummate proof that he intends to return to the same failed policies that took America, and our economy straight over a cliff!

Jim Green

Letter to the editor/President
Obama/Fellow Democrats:

THE HISTORY OF HOW WE GOT WHERE WE ARE:

In the mid-1970's, the colliding forces of automation, technology, globalization, etc., reached a critical mass, resulting in ubiquitous unemployment in all of the OECD countries, and has left their leaders conflicted, ever since, regarding the displaced employee—Eurozone unemployment is still in double digits, with Spain at 22.9%.

In the U.S., we took a pro-active role in addressing this economic shift—and in 1978 President Carter signed into law 15 USC § 3101--which "authorizes" the creation of a "reservoir of public employment" at any time our unemployment in America exceeds "3%".

In 1979, however, and in a panic over Humphrey-Hawkins—our ultra-conservative foundations, and desperate to preserve the "market only" job creation concept, embraced a flawed paper by an obscure MIT student, David L. Birch "The Job Generation Process"; and [with lots of cash] gave his paper biblical importance, and every president since has cited his finding as gospel.

Birch's paper concluded that "small businesses" were the greatest generator of new jobs—problem is, for the purposes of policy-making—it is BS. In a study at Harvard University in 2010, "The Myth of Small Business Job Creation" The research shows "no systematic relationship between firm size and growth." And that small businesses can actually detract from job growth.

In spite of this, however, Washington struggles, still, to make this antiquated notion, work--that it is only the market that can create jobs—and the result has been a disaster, politically as well as otherwise!

It would be impossible to still have 8.2% unemployment—if we were on the right path—and among other problems with this concept--if the market fails, the unemployed are out of luck.

Further, unemployment is a "social" problem we are seeking to address with a highly unstable, incompatible entity: The Market

What apparently isn't clear going forward is that an expanding and contracting public workforce is an INDISPENSABLE component to the correct functioning of a modern market economy—

The market thrives when we have a robust, employed, consuming workforce—and overlooked is that HR 870 [currently in Committee], and the proposed "Neighbor-To-Neighbor Job Creation Act" www.Inclusivism.org [both authorized under Humphrey-Hawkins], are deficit-neutral--Pro-Market "win-win" solutions.

The American people win, and capitalism wins—

Jim Green, Democrat candidate for Congress, 2000

To the editor:

A Republican candidate for president said "On next January 20, there will begin in Washington, the biggest unraveling, unsnarling, untangling operation in our nation's history."

But before rank and file Republicans say "right on" regarding President Obama— this was from an archive speech by Republican candidate Tom Dewey, and directed at President Truman, in 1948.

Will politics never change? Given the political rhetoric you would think President Truman couldn't even tie his own shoes—albeit, he had ended WWII [while President Obama has rescued America from another Great Depression].

And other parallels between these two elections are even more striking.

For instance, Truman was outraged by what he called a "Do nothing Congress"—and he went on the warn the electorate that "The country cannot afford another Republican Congress." Are we in an echo chamber, here?

The most startling parallel, however, is when Truman said of the Republican

Congress on a stump speech "It is a sad tale of the sell out of the American people to these gluttons of privilege— these cold men who skim the cream from our natural resources to satisfy their own greed."

This could have been said yesterday, and yet, it was said by President Truman 64 years ago!

Finally, President Truman offered some words of wisdom to the American electorate on the danger of returning our government back to the Republicans [as true today, as then] "I'm just waking you up to the fact that this is YOUR fight—and YOU are going to be the loser [if you return the White House back to the Republicans]."

And, as every student of History knows, and in spite of the inexcusable headline error by the Chicago Tribune "DEWEY DEFEATS TRUMAN"—President Truman won.

Jim Green

Letter to editor:

A number of our new congresspersons are threatening to dismantle the healthcare reforms by the Democrats [which actually didn't go far enough]— but we need to ask, why on earth would they even consider doing this?

The only persons complaining about the reforms made by Democrats to our healthcare system—are persons who do not understand the healthcare system we have now [and this can also be said about many of the reforms over the past 2 years]—

For instance, America is the only country in the world that permits their health insurance companies to make a "profit" off of people getting healthcare—

After all, our health insurance companies don't even so much as put a Band-Aid on a patient—they are simply a pass-through agent—and in a "for profit" system it is impossible to remove the "cut services to increase profits" syndrome—it is bedrock capitalism—

And which works selling used cars, but is a horrid concept re the health of humans, and has resulted in "death panels" by greedy health insurance companies—and rumors of canceling policies while a subscriber is on a gurney awaiting surgery!

We pool our money to brace against the high costs of healthcare, if we need it [as with all other insurance] and they pay out our claims--[and as a footnote, identical in concept to paying taxes—where we pool our money for our individual protection, and for the common good]--

As it has turned out our health insurance companies have turned this "pass through" thing they do—not just into a way to make a little money in the process—but rather into a Texas-sized bonanza---a gold mine at the expense of our health--this is not a big business—it is a big, big, big business—with obscene salaries for their CEO's—and a cumulative $300 billion in "profits"—not a dime of which goes to the healthcare of anyone!

For instance, our health insurance companies have six lobbyists for each of the 435 Members of Congress, and 100 members of the Senate—all with six figure salaries--as I write—and all are there for only one reason—to protect the pot of gold the health insurance companies are making off of the American people!

But the real wake-up call—for those who do not understand the reforms made by the Democrats—every dime of those salaries to lobbyists came from money they sent in in premiums—money intended for the healthcare of Americans, not to enrich the health insurance companies!

This also explains why we are 37th in the world in the quality of healthcare in America, according to the World Health Organization—and we have a mortality rate along side some Third World countries!

In sum—and for clarity---sell a car, make a buck—absolutely, this is the America way—but making a "profit" off of people's health should be a criminal offense—

Jim Green

Letter to Editor:

RE: Republican House refusing to raise the debt ceiling--

The "or else" warning from Republicans to Democrats this past week is a grim warning that America is on its way out as a Super Power [yes, I know this sounds like the scare tactics The Heritage Foundation is notorious for, but]-- hear me out—

First the "or else" message is devoid of subtlety—it was a specific statement to support their one and only program "To make their richest contributors, richer"—or else we will block everything you are doing—regardless of the Americans who will be injured in he process!

In the first place, their "or else" was thumbing their nose at 98% of those who vote Republican because they are crystal clear that they represent the top 2%---PERIOD.

That is, they do not represent what is in the best interest of 98% of Americans— they represent what is in the best interest of the their richest contributors—PERIOD!

In short, there is night and day between the rank and file who vote Republican—and the national Republican Party, and specific here to: The Republicans in Congress—

For instance, the rank and file Republican overwhelmingly supports reducing the deficit—but the "or else" warning from the Republicans in Congress insists upon increasing our deficit [so their richest contributors, can get richer]1

Here is a test for understanding what the Republicans in Congress are up to: Add the words "To make my richest

contributors, richer" to every word they
utter, or every piece of legislation they
propose—and you will have a
consummate understanding what they
mean--when their lips are moving, as
well as their proposed legislation—

In short, folks, the sheer gall in this
warning tells us, sadly, that we are on
our way out—

Jim Green

To the editor:

The only way any person could "condemn" the way President Obama is handling the job—are persons who have not informed themselves with the facts—or are suffering from severe amnesia—or both—

Republican policies had handed President Obama an economy in shambles when he took office in 2009— and we had lost 2.6 million jobs in 2008, alone, the highest job loss in six decades!

We can't siphon America's wealth out of the hands of the consuming middle, the 99%--and transfer it into the hands of the Republican's wealthiest contributors, the 1% [via obscene tax cuts]—without sending our economy into meltdown.

This is based on common sense—The consuming middle stops buying the products made by our manufacturers, when they don't have enough money—and in the domino effect our manufacturers lay off their employees when they don't have consumers for their products—and on and on until our economy is in shambles.

And those who inform themselves know that Reaganomics [what Bush I called "VooDoo economics] has a shelf-life of about seven years before the economy collapses—as it did in 1987, and again in 2008—

And the taxpayers have to rush in with tons of cash, as Bush did with TARP in 2008, and an equal amount by President Obama--to prevent another Great Depression.

Also, with each new cycle of this economic scheme—the bail out has grown larger and larger—

For instance, in 1987—when the stock market lost one-fourth of its value on Black Monday, October 19, 1987—the bailout was in the hundreds of billions—in 2008, the bailout has been in the trillions of dollars, and counting--to mop up the mess caused by this failed economic agenda!

In short, President Obama did not spend the tons of cash [and as Bush did with TARP]—because he is a wild "tax and spend" liberal—and as our racists and Republican ideologues would have our uninformed believe—

Both Obama and Bush went to the only doctor in town for a prescription [cash and plenty of it] to rescue America from another Great Depression!

Further, when any of the Republicans in Washington rail against our deficit, who voted to cause it—as Paul Ryan did under Bush II—is a hypocrite!

Romney has made it clear, in no uncertain terms, that he intends to pickup where Bush II left off—i.e., to pander to the GREED of the Republican's richest contributors at the expense of the 99% rest of us—it is the Republican One and Only program—

And the rank and file would do well to heed the warning by President Truman in 1948—that it is us, the American people, who will be the "loser" if we fail to inform ourselves and return America to "VooDoo Economics"!

Jim Green

To the Editor:

Someone needs to respond to the editorial [SG 1-14-11] "Politics doesn't answer the 'why' " re the Tuscon massacre in which a member of Congress was shot—

The level of inflammatory political vitriol has been a matter of concern in America, long before this shooting—and like a computer game based on violence—in each new version the violence is kicked up a gear—

And over the past two years civil discourse in politics has virtually disappeared and/or been replaced with this vitriolic diatribe—and "politics" has ceased to be about creating a better America, in the best interest of the American people—and is solely about "getting elected"--

Over the past week, Sarah Palin has, inexplicably and incredulously, tried to portray herself as the victim and to distance herself from her "cross-hairs" program to target Democrats in the 2010 election [including the Congresswoman]—as well as many other Republicans—

But, the bottom line is—that while we do not have enough evidence, yet, to say with certainty that these inflammatory remarks incited an unstable, mentally ill person, to violence—we also do not have enough evidence to say that it didn't—and that being the case—we all need to work together to end this destructive trend in our political dialogue--ASAP!

Jim Green

Letter to the editor/My Republican Friends--

I never ceased to be amazed how few persons who vote Republican—actually know what the national Republican Party is up to—

Which is to move as much cash as they can from their pocket—and move it into the pockets of their richest contributors—the 400 persons who currently hold more of America's wealth than 150 million of the rest of us do!

Several questions may offer some insight. Why did the Republicans in

Congress have a temper tantrum re the mere 4% increase—as the tax cuts for the top 2% were about to expire on 12-31-11?

Why has the Republican Party inundated the airwaves with a blizzard of Red Herring propaganda ads from gays marrying to anti-choice? HINT: To get us to talk about everything under the sun—except that they have their hand in our pocket!

And why does the current Republican Congress want to slash and burn programs for our children—and even a $4.43 Billion cut in veteran benefits?

The national Republican Party supports "smaller government" for only one reason—so that their richest contributors don't have to pay any taxes!

And their strategy for making their richest contributors richer—is by shifting the payment of taxes from the 2%--to the 98% rest of us! Thus the temper tantrum last December—

A couple of final points—since 1980 we have had the greatest shift of wealth from the consuming 98%, to the top 2%--in American history—and as history has also taught us this siphoning of wealth from the consuming middle has resulted in a collapse of the economy –1987 & 2008.

Further, since 1980 we have had tons of tax watchdog groups cropping up all over the place—speaking of the evil of taxes--some by persons who would starve to death if others didn't pay theirs—[

Lost in all of this is the only question all of us Americans should be asking: What kind of America do we want for ourselves?

And Americans spoke with one voice in the 2008 election: Fix Unemployment!

Further, in 1840 we agreed that we wanted our children educated; and in the 30's we agreed that we did not want our seniors lining our streets with "Will Work For Food" signs—true of many Third World counties!

Finally,, anyone who thinks this is just another Democrat ideologue—would be wrong—we got half a loaf on hospitalization—rather than a real fix—and President Obama got bad advice re how to fix unemployment—with 9-17%

unemployed as proof! But then, half a loaf is better than none--

Jim Green, Democrat candidate for Congress, 2000 www.Inclusivism.org

[This letter is something I never intended to do when I started out—but it is chocked full of facts every informed voter, rich or poor, should read twice, daily, until the election. It is a letter from former Congressman [and current candidate] Alan Grayson, from Florida, who was swept into office in 2008, and swept out in 2010—when the Koch brothers spent a quarter of a million dollars to defeat his re-election— because he is a "truth-teller"—and if there is anything the Republicans cannot stand—it is someone who blows the whistle on their scams]1

"A few weeks ago, it was reported that some right-wing rich guys' club had pledged $100 million to defeat President Obama. The Koch Brothers led the way, pledging $60 mil. Which is pocket change, when your net worth is $50,000,000,000.00.

Leaving aside the obvious issue – the estate tax – I'm puzzled as to why all those right-wing rich folks feel that way. The foundation of their wealth – the stock market – has performed vastly better when Democrats have been in charge.

In 2008, the New York Times reported that since 1929, $10,000 invested in the stock market under Democratic Presidents (over 40 years) had become $300,671. Meanwhile, $10,000 invested in the stock market under Republican Presidents (over 35 years) had become only $11,733.

Well, at least the affluent caste didn't *lose* money during Republican regimes, right? Wrong. The value of the dollar dropped by 92% during that period. So in real value, $10,000 invested in the stock market under Republican Presidents actually became just $955. And forty-six cents. In economic terms, roughly the same effect as some foreign enemy blowing up 90% of our factories, warehouses, farms, malls, office buildings, apartment buildings, and every other productive asset.

Poor rich people. All the money gone. Those darned Republicans.

And under President Obama, the difference actually has increased, dramatically. On the day that President Obama was sworn into office, the S&P 500 index closed at 805. Today, it's at 1321. Under President Obama, the stock market is up 64%, in less than four years.

That brings the Democratic average annual stock market performance up to 10%. The Republican figure is 0.4%. No wonder Republicans hate government – they're so bad at it. Particularly when it comes preserving national wealth.

And despite the incessant whining of the corporate rich, by no stretch of the imagination are they suffering under the Obama Administration. Just today, it was reported that pay for CEOs has reached an all-time high, just short of $10 million a year. Or roughly $5,000 an hour. Good work, if you can get it.

So why are all these right-wing deep pockets going after Obama and the Democrats? Even if you're some selfish rich guy, that's just dumb. That's cutting your wallet to spite your pants. Maybe the rich need to develop a little class consciousness.

Honestly, when you look at the facts, these robber barons spending huge wads of cash to get rid of the Democrats are like lemmings. They're all jumping off the money cliff, and they're taking everyone else with them.

Most of us have heard the question, "If you're so smart, why aren't you rich?"

But a better question would be, "If you're so rich, why aren't you smart?"

Courage, Alan Grayson"

To the editor:

I am genuinely concerned about the "wedge" issues being used to sabotage our elections! A large part of the problem is what I call the "literal logic" applied by religious extremists.

Under literal logic if even one of the building blocks which holds their logic system together is found to be untrue....the entire logic system falls apart, and thus they "invent" reasons, some of which defy all human reasoning, to make the "flawed" building block true.

For instance, rather than accepting that each of the six days God took to create the earth, could represent millions of years each....the literal logic folks, say, nope....it is literally our 24 hour day.

And thus to make the 24 hour day idea work, they argue that the earth came into existence about 4000 years ago....give or take....[And most in the Tea Party, including Senator Paul, actually believe this stuff!] .

Also, to make it all work they assert that man walked the earth at the same time as dinosaurs, which even our Kindergartners understand existed millions of years ago (i.e., why we have oil)...and yet the literal logic folks cling to the 24 hour idea to the last burning ember….to make their logic system work!

All of this would be laughable to anyone who is rational, but the fact is these folks now have "political capital"….and they are determined to "spend it"! The truth is, the damage they are doing to our young minds is irrelevant to these extremists!

And The sad result is 37 of our state legislatures currently have some form of legislation (call it "creationism" or "intelligent design" --an oxymoron in this context if their ever was one) to teach our kids that "By God, 24 hours, means 24 hours"!

I thought we settled the evolution issue 80 years ago….at the Scopes Trial? (There are a whole bunch of reasons why the literal logic folks don't like evolution, but space doesn't permit)

The sad fact is, folks, our country is going backwards…as the rest of the world is racing headlong into the future as a result of the extremists trying to foist their political agenda off on the rest of us….and America is becoming the laughing stock around the world.

For instance, Canada made the "morning after" pill available over the counter, and recently they made same sex marriages legal. Championing individual freedoms used to be our forte, but no more....now they are used as "wedge issues" to take control of our political agenda!

There is a word for what is happening to America....it is called "entropy"....when a country collapses, not by external forces such as terrorists (they should be the least of our worries), but rather by internal forces....and a tiny minority at that.....intent upon foisting their political agenda off on the rest of us!

But unless we start speaking up in America and drown out the wedge propaganda nonsense in this election-

– America is are going to be
steamrollered into the Stone Age!

Jim Green

To the editor.

A few years back Peter Drucker wrote a book entitled ""The Age of Discontinuity" and today we are living the concept on steroids—where virtually every person who votes Republican—doesn't have a clue to what the Republican "leadership" is up to—

We have a representative government— i.e., we hire people to represent what is in our best interest—and the Republican "leadership" could care less what is in the best interest of 99% of those who voted for them!

They represent what is in the best interest of their richest contributors—and if you are not in that tiny handful of Americans, then they have their hand in YOUR pocket to get money to give to their richest contributors!

In short, if you are not worth half a billion dollars, or more—and you are voting Republican—you need to have your head examined [and given the larger picture-it is even dumb for these folks]!

Indeed, from the first day Reagan took office, until Bush II left office the Republican "leadership" oversaw the greatest transfer of wealth—out of the hands of the masses and into the hands of their richest contributors [the top 1%] – in the history of America—and it was solely to pander to the greed of the top 1% [it has never been about building a better and stronger America]!

In a nutshell—the Republican "leadership" is not even within a country mile of representing what is in the best interest of those who blindly voted for them--

To illustrate, Mitt Romney's speeches are a metaphor for the Republican agenda—which is glued together with half-truths, glittering generalities—and flat out lies…..and all disguised to cover up their true, and One and Only program.

To make their richest contributors, richer—Period! That's it, Folks----it is the sum total of what they stand for--

And all one needs to do is to add the words "To make our richest contributors, richer"—to every word uttered, or piece of legislation introduced by the Republican "leadership"--and you will have a consummate understanding of this utterances or legislation!

Jim Green

[Dear Reader: The following isn't a letter to the editor—and if you have gotten this far—I have questioned including it here—let alone sent to a newspaper—but it needs to be said…..]

A MESSAGE FROM GOD

MANY CENTURIES AGO, a man of the cloth, we don't know his name, and in a flash of insight (perhaps induced by peyote) told his flock that "sex is a sin". And lo and behold he learned that by taking a very natural and healthy part of our life and turning it into something that was "dirty and nasty", that he could imprison his flock, and fill his coffers, and hallelujah it was a great day for the Lord!

Quickly, his miracle spread to other churches in his village, and then to the next village, and then the next county and then state and then it spread to all the churches in the ancient world, and all of their flocks cowed in fear and shame and became imprisoned, and their coffers over-floweth. Hallelujah, it was a great day for the Lord!

And to keep the myth alive they started inventing stories, half-baked stories, that made no sense to anyone who is rational, such as "Mary was a virgin"—well, she just had to be a virgin because she would never partake in anything that was dirty and nasty, like sex (if you're doing it right), and this was necessary to make "sex is a sin" make sense...so they invented a Mary that was "sinless"--you get the picture. And their coffers over-floweth. Hallelujah, it was a great day for the Lord!

No one seemed to be bothered that when we play tricks on the human mind by taking something that is very natural and healthy, such as sex, and make it dirty and nasty that all kinds of bad things happen to the human mind.

Such as most pedophiles, and most serial killers, and voting Republican, and unwarranted suicides, and most mental illness, and unwanted pregnancies. (Teens not wanting to have sex is the perversion, not the other way around, and by replacing sex education and condoms, with unrealistic "abstinence", and by using blather about "low self-esteem" to shame them into not "sinning"--We have a teen pregnancy in the U.S. twice that of England and Canada!).

But none of this mattered, because their coffers over-floweth, and Hallelujah, it is a great day for the Lord!

There is a cure--------Tell these right-wing loonies to shove it....

GOD

To the editor:

A question critical to America's well being is not being asked today—but it should be given only the highest priority by our politicians.

Does the American government have a responsibility to step up to the plate, when the market is not providing enough jobs?

And we need to keep in mind, under our Constitution—WE the American people are the "government"—

So to drill down on this a bit, what is really being asked is should we, the American people, act on our own behalf regarding our unemployment crisis—

And the American people have answered that with a resounding YES—

Indeed, every politician in the past century has proclaimed: "Anybody wanting to work, should be able to find a job"—this quote is from President Obama, as reported to him by thousands of voters.

There is no lack of clarity regarding what WE, the American want regarding jobs.

And it is the most important economic/social/political issue facing America, today—and particularly "political" in that no president has been re-elected when we have high unemployment.

Part of what is missing in the discussion is that employment is a "social" problem—and thus our "government" has a SOLEMN responsibility to step in when the market does not provide enough jobs—

A point lost in our current antiquated
economic solutions—which still have
one foot on the plantation—

The world has changed, our solutions
haven't, and the result has been a
disaster!

It would be impossible to have 25
million Americans unemployed, or
underemployed—if the path we are
currently on actually worked---the data
is our evidence—

The fact is, the question above is not
new to America—and has been on the

books for 65 years--with President
Truman signing the "Full Employment
Act of 1946" to assure employment for
our troops following WW II—

So why is it not part of our political
dialogue, today?

Jim Green

To the editor/An open letter to Ali Velshi.

Ali Velshi, CNN's economic guru—goes apoplectic over the suggestion that we should use "public employment" to solve our unemployment crisis—

He is not alone—what we loosely call "conventional wisdom" clings to this concept, and whenever our media reports the latest employment figures— they are always quick to add "private-sector jobs"—as if there is an extra cookie in it for making the distinction from the horrible alternative --"public sector jobs"—

It would be ideal if the market could absorb everyone in—provide a job to anybody wanting to work—but it never has, and it never will—

First, because employment is only incidental to the market, not the objective—and fixing unemployment is antithetical to its objectives—[it is the reason our corporations are sitting on $2 trillion in cash]

Indeed, when every waking moment in capitalism is spent pondering ways to eliminate as many of us humans as possible, from the workplace, to increase profits---why on earth would anyone rational look to the market to solve such a critical social problem?

Looking to the market to solve our unemployment crisis is analogous to going to a barbershop to buy pork chops--

Which brings us to the question—why is there so much resistance to "public employment"? Why does "conventional wisdom" speak of "public sector jobs" as if they were the plague?

And we need to drill down on that and ask Ali Velshi, [all persons who harbor this belief], to state SPECIFICALLY their resistance to "public employment"?

Work—by definition, is "being a productive human being"—and the larger question is--is this a universal human need—i.e., is there a case for this being a human right?

It is a question that panics "conventional wisdom"—and the question is WHY?

Also, ignored is the fact that unemployment is a "social" problem which clearly puts it under the province of government to solve--

Ironically, we have a narrow body of law in America--going back 65 years—that is very specific that government ["We the people"]—have an absolute responsibility to step up with "public sector jobs", when the market falls short [15 USC § 3101, HR 870, currently in Committee]

In closing, if this question or subject seems irrelevant—America, today, runs a real risk of President Obama being replaced with an idiot—because we have not solved the problem of unemployment--

So, Mr. Velshi, et al—please answer the question—THX

Jim Green, Democrat candidate for Congress, 2000   www.Inclusivism.org

To the editor/An open letter to Republicans in Congress

A Unique Solution: Fix Unemployment-Fix Economy

The perception is that Washington is focused on ending our unemployment crisis—but is it really?

Never, in any of the proposed solutions by the Republicans, have our laws been based on the premise: Fix Unemployment-Fix Economy

Indeed, it apparently, has not even been raised to the level of consciousness—

and ALL of the Republican solutions are framed around. Fix the economy and this will in turn fix our unemployment crisis—[the Republicans in Congress are incapable of thinking otherwise]--

And in spite of the fact that.

1] This path has barely moved the unemployment needle down—

2] It will take 7 years just to get back to even 5% unemployment [our current full employment norm]—

3] It ignores the American people who believe that "anybody wanting to work should be able to find a job"—

4] It ignores that the market thrives when we have a robust, employed, consuming workforce—[indeed, the Republican solution is an anti-market path to follow]--

5] And finally, under this premise--if the market fails, the unemployed are out of luck—

So why do we keep insisting, where being an "employee" is concerned, that humans are without "rights", and to be beholden to the whims of the market?

Dr. David Ewing, former editor of the Harvard Business Review—penned in his book , "Freedom Inside The Organization", that "Employee rights are like a black hole in space, so impacted by tradition that light can barely escape".

And best guess is that it is a "sacred cow", and an error in our thinking about the market concept—

Specifically, that humans are seen as a "commodity" in the market, and that the market will only work if humans are to be used and discarded "at will"—a concept that fails to understand the true nature of man.

When "conventional wisdom" had it that the world was flat—world travel was out of the question—and the same self-limiting mind-set is in play, here—IMHO

On a positive note, we could be a beacon of light to all of the OECD countries—[which appear to be laboring under the same "sacred cow"]—by signing into law the proposed "Neighbor-To-Neighbor Job Creation Act".

A deficit–neutral, federally mandated mutual insurance, owned by our employed [from janitor to CEO]—to provide a fund to hire/train our unemployed— www.Inclusivism.org — See also, 15 USC § 3101, and HR 870 [currently in Committee].

Jim Green, Democrat candidate for Congress, 2000

To the editor:

ABC News recently had a segment celebrating contractors who built homes made 100% from products "Made In America"—which every American can agree 110%.

The problem with this segment, however, is that it did not deal with the underlying problem:

As a result of automation, alone, since the mid-1970's, the market has been creating fewer and fewer jobs in all of the OECD countries, and this phenomenon will only become more pronounced the further we move into the 21st Century—

And yet, we keep insisting on a "Market Only" fix to our unemployment crisis in America—

It is reminiscent of the scene from "Young Frankenstein" when Igor—in response to a question about his hump back—he replied "What hump?

The phenomenon is real—but we appear to have our head buried in the sand and have framed all of our solutions around the Market fixing the problem—if it takes forever—[current projections show that under the best of circumstances--it will take 7 years just to get back to 5% unemployment].

The question we should have on the table is: Does the government have the responsibility to step up, on behalf of American people, when the market does not create enough jobs—

But in a "denial" scenario—the question is not even on the table.

The irony in all of this is that 34 years ago, in 1978, and almost to the day— America responded directly to this phenomenon—

Specifically, Congress passed and President Carter signed into law 15 USC § 3101--which "authorizes" the creation of a "reservoir of public employment" at any time our unemployment in America exceeds "3%".

To implement this concept my proposed solution
 [at www.Inclusivism.org] is the Neighbor-To-Neighbor Job Creation Act: A federally mandated mutual insurance, owned by our employed [from janitor to CEO], to provide a fund

to hire/train our unemployed—and without adding a dime to our deficit!

Public sector jobs beget private sector jobs, and for a modest policy cost of 4% of salary we could create more private sector jobs in 6 months, than our current path in 6 years [HR 2847], and end our unemployment crisis within a year of passage.

Incidentally, this solution to end our unemployment crisis is "Made In America"—

Jim Green

To the editor:

According to Charles Darwin we evolve [grow] by adapting to our environment—and conversely under this theory, species [or nations] that fail to adapt become extinct—

And in applying this to "High and persistent unemployment has pervaded almost every OECD country since the mid-1970's."—we keep insisting on applying a solution that doesn't work, and rather than adapting to a world that has changed—our refusal to adapt, has resulted in a disastrous result, political and otherwise.

The quote, above, is by an internationally recognized economist, as well as an abundance of data which every credible economist agrees with—albeit, they differ on the reason[s] why.

In short, it would be impossible to have an 8.2% unemployment rate if we were on the right path.

At the core of the problem is an innate human need that is not being recognized. The need to be a productive human—it is linked to "self-preservation"-- and which in modern society is the human need to "work".

Conservatives/Republicans believe that "humans are lazy and don't want to work"—when exactly the opposite is true—and a point lost on Republicans is that the "welfare bum" is OUR creation, not theirs--

But because of this lapse in our evolution all of our solutions to unemployment have been framed around the market solving the problem—i.e., and excuse the honesty, but the American employee is seen as a "commodity in a pool of slaves" to be used and discarded "at will".

In short, in terms of social evolution--
our adaptation to a world that has
changed—we are barely off the
plantation.

Our solution both undermines the
market, as well as the unemployed—The
market thrives when we have a robust,
employed, consuming workforce—

And it is our being beholden to the
mind-set, above, that has barely moved
the unemployment needle down—and
the pervasive high unemployment may
well result in the unthinkable—it may
cost President Obama re-election.

In sum, the world has changed, our solutions haven't, and the result has been a disaster—

And the really sad fact is that we have had the solution for ending our unemployment dilemma at our fingertips since 1978—15 USC § 3101 [as well as HR 870—currently in Committee], but because of the above lapse in our social evolution—it has been over-looked or simply not understood—

The problem, of course, in getting out too far ahead with a fundamental truth

gets one written off as a crackpot—so be
it--

Jim Green

To the editor/An open letter to Fellow Democrats:

According to Professor Lakoff, a linguist at the University of California—we Democrats have failed "to understand the difference between policy and morality, that morality beats policy, and that moral discourse is absolutely necessary." He asserts that this is a major reason we lost the House in 2010.

Bush used the public's money to increase our government by a third, and "corporate welfare" and "privatization scams" --are socialist concepts--

And in response to Republican claims that they are "Pro-Market"—it is BS—the Republicans have obfuscated their One and Only program to confuse the electorate. To pander to the GREED of their wealthiest contributors – by claiming this is "Pro-Market" –

When, in fact, it is solely to transfer the wealth from the consuming middle to the 1%, and put the short-fall in revenue on the tab for the American taxpayer to pay—a socialist concept, and, of course, it drove our economy over a cliff—AND AT THE EXPENSE OF THE MARKET!

More businesses have failed when the Republicans held the White House, than at any other time in our history!

Yes, this is preaching to the choir, but when it comes to "values" the Democrats have a sterling record—so why is the public perception otherwise [thanks to the lying, liars in the Republican Party]?

So when are going to start a campaign to correct the record? And calling the Republicans Anti-Christian/Socialists is a good start—and when are we going to identify Paul Ryan and Limbaugh, et al, by what they are --"Not decent people"?

But most important, we need to listen to George Lakoff by expressing and repeating Democrat Moral Values – Often--

Jim Green, Democrat candidate for Congress, 2000   www.Inclusivism.org YouTube: JGREEN56789

To the editor:

Washington can be divided into two camps, today—those who don't know how to solve our unemployment crisis— and those who are indifferent to the problem--

For instance, the Republicans in Congress actually believe the fairytale they are peddling to the public—[their one and only job creation program, i.e., just cut taxes for their wealthiest contributors and this will magically translate into jobs]—

If this actually worked—what is their explanation for our having 14-25 million Americans still unemployed?

The Tax Cuts Were Extended! Their solution to our unemployment crisis is in place! It isn't working!

Most likely, the vast majority of Republicans know this is a canard—are indifferent to the plight of our unemployed Americans—and the big money says they will do everything they can to undermine any effective solution by Democrats—for purely "political" reasons—

And it is a sorry state--but for the majority of Republicans in Congress it is Tricky-Dick Politics "10"—What will make a better and stronger America "0"—

So this leaves us with those in Washington who do not know how to solve our unemployment crisis—

And perhaps least understood is that the vast majority of American workers want to chip in to help their neighbor go back to work—and why this generosity is not incorporated in a "win-win" solution to our unemployment crisis defies rational human thought—

Specifically, the Senate needs to pass a proposed "Neighbor-To-Neighbor Job Creation Act"—a deficit neutral, federally mandated, mutual insurance [similar to Social Security Insurance] owned by every employed person in America--to provide the funds to hire/train our unemployed—and then challenge the House Republicans to explain why they voted against jobs! See: www.Inclusivism.org

Further, we need to embrace as our model the Humphrey-Hawkins Full Employment Act, and the current version of Humphrey-Hawkins by Rep.

Conyers-- HR 870 [in Committee—and also deficit neutral] – which authorizes "a reservoir of public employment" anytime our jobless rate rises above "3%".

We have far more jobs that need to be done in America—in every jurisdiction in America—than we have persons to fill these jobs—and the market thrives when we have a robust, employed, workforce!

In short, this is a "win-win" solution—the American people win, and capitalism wins!

Jim Green

To the editor:

All of the data shows "High and persistent unemployment has pervaded almost every OECD country since the mid-1970s." A quote, and documented in a paper by Dr. William F. Mitchell, Director of the Department of Economics, University of Newcastle, Australia.

In a stroke of genius, and led by former Vice-President Hubert Humphrey, America responded to this phenomenon in 1978, when Congress passed, and President Carter signed into law 15 USC § 3101--which "authorizes" the creation of a "reservoir of public employment" at any time our unemployment in America exceeds "3%".

Dr. Mitchell, and also in response to the phenomenon, later presented a paper at the University of Chicago, in which he outlined the Buffer Stock Employment Model. An expanding and contracting public workforce—that expands during downturns in the market, and contracts as employees return to the private sector.

Both answer the question: Does a government have the responsibility to step in when the market does not provide enough jobs with a resounding, Yes.

And, this is a particularly relevant and essential solution in all of the 30 market-driven, OECD countries, including America.

The fact is, our unemployment rate in America should at no time exceed 3%, and even more relevant is the fact that the market thrives when we have a robust, employed, consuming public—

In short, the government stepping up with public sector jobs is a Pro-Market, win-win solution—the citizens win, and capitalism wins—

So why do we have this lapse in our social evolution? Why have we chosen "lose-lose", over "win-win"?

It is more than the cost causing our paralysis—we can fund without adding a dime to our deficit—HR 870 [currently in Committee in the House], and the proposed Neighbor-To-Neighbor Job Creation Act" [www.Inclusivism.org], just to name two—

The only logical deduction is that. Myths and sacred cows have stood in the way of implementation of this solution-- even in the face of mass unemployment, and to the economic/social/political detriment of America.

For one, the sad fact is, the current "market" mind-set still has one foot on the plantation—the "employee" is perceived as being drawn from a "pool of slaves" to be used and discarded "at will"—[why else would "at will" employment be so prevalent in America?]—and regardless of how civilized we claim to be—

And the above solution threatens this sacred cow, and archaic mind-set—IMHO

Jim Green

To the editor:

WHAT WOULD HAPPEN IF "WE THE
PEOPLE" [The Government] STEPPED IN
WHEN THE MARKET DID NOT
PROVIDE ENOUGH JOBS.

"The country demands bold, persistent
experimentation, it is common sense to
take a method and try it....if it fails,
admit it frankly and try another, but
above all, try something!" President
Franklin Roosevelt, 1933

I am a capitalist. I would hope that
everyone could invent a better mouse
trap, sell it for a million dollars, and

retire in the Bahamas. The flaw in the capitalist's system is that it sees humans as a "commodity" rather than a "resource", and when left to its own devices it creates enormous inequities.

A blind spot in provincial thinking re capitalism is that it requires "trickle up" policies to make it work...and rather than being a "tax burden" (a conservative buzz term to pander to greed) it is, in fact an essential ingredient in making capitalism work. And a prime example is that we have not had another Great Depression since the implementation of Social Security—

and it is the only reason we are not in one now!

The greatest lapse in our thinking, however, is in not recognizing "work" as a "human right". That is, a right held by every citizen of legal age. The framework for implementing this "bold experimentation" can be found at www.Inclusivism.org.

AMENDED. IF WORK, THE RIGHT TO BE A PRODUCTIVE HUMAN, BECAME THE "LEGAL RIGHT" OF EACH CITIZEN OF LEGAL AGE—WHAT WOULD HAPPEN?

First, an "employment insurance" would be established to provide employment to the unemployed. Our unemployment offices would become employment offices, and work could not be denied to any citizen who applies.

At present there is a superficial interest on the part of our unemployment offices in finding work for the unemployed— but by an large they are another of our antiquated Police State solutions, and they see their real role as acting as a police agency in denying claims to save money for "employers", corporate and public, and to be vigilant in checking up to see that unemployment recipients are not cheating. Most believe that the recipients are lazy and don't want to work.

All of this, including the erroneous assumptions about humans, would disappear—because the need for unemployment payments, as well as most of our current welfare system, would disappear-- and the saved income would be returned to an "employment insurance" pool set up to provide employment for the unemployed.

Also in this pool would be the income from the same "insurance" fund and which every employed person would pay into—to provide employment.

This insurance would be federally mandated, much the same as Social Security Insurance, but unlike Social Security Insurance certain groups, such as some school districts and government agencies, including federal employees could not opt out of the system, and enrollment would be mandatory—even for the president---with the enrollment fee set up on a graduated scale.

Every person who works would pay into the insurance in the interest of providing employment to those who are unemployed.

And while there may a disgruntled soul here and there (who does not want their money used to employ someone who is black, or brown, or old—there always is) it is speculated that this would be wildly applauded by the vast majority in the interest of the larger society—or in their own self-interest.

The lesson from Social Security Insurance is that we have not had another Great Depression since it was implemented in 1935, and that Social Security and Military Retirement moneys, etc., trickling up through our economy is most likely the reason we are not in one now. In short, finding work to be a "legal right" is a "win-win" proposition, and it cannot be ignored that Bill Gates became the richest man in the world, in large part, as a result of these funds percolating up through our economy.

There are currently 8,800 pending state infrastructure programs seeking funding in the respective states, so there is hardly a shortage of employment opportunities. Our emphasis, of course, should be on those projects which will make America energy independent and on protecting the environment.

And we should not rule out allowing the owners of the, above, "employment insurance" to vote on national projects—such as a high speed rail system, etc., ---and dividends would be paid to the owners of the employment insurance from unused funds. This is, after all, not a tax----it is an insurance plan.

Finally, it cannot be stressed strongly enough that this is a "right" held by the individual citizen. It is possible that no citizen would seek to exercise this right…and that would be fine. The right to work and be a productive citizen was a given in primitive societies, but lost in the age of industrialization and advent of the corporation. In short, it is neither compulsory, nor is it welfare—and in the end it may have more of a psychological, than economic impact—because over time it will change the way we look at each other.

Jim Green, Democrat candidate for Congress, Dist 21, TX, 2000
www.Inclusivism.org

To the editor:

SOLVING OUR UNEMPLOYMENT
CRISIS WITH WISHFUL THINKING....

We have yet to deal with unemployment
in America. Unemployment relates to
individuals who are "unemployed"--it is
a "social" problem--it is an everyday, not
someday problem for the unemployed...

We have used tax cuts, tax incentives
and cash to our corporations [HR 2847,
Reaganomics] to jump-start our
economy--on the promise that jobs will
result--but it is nothing more than that,
and ending unemployment is incidental

to this mind-set--NOT specific to the problem of unemployment--

Producing jobs is based on wishful thinking that the market will fix our unemployment crisis--

The world has changed, our solutions haven't, and we have created a Police State in America to hold our antiquated solutions in place....

Our current methodology has multiple flaws:

1] While appearing to be pro-capitalism, it is, in fact, anti-capitalism-

-it is harmful to a modern market economy.

2] It is asking the "Market" to solve a problem, that is antithetical to its objectives--the market is in the "for profit" business, not in the "social work" business--and would soon be out of business under the latter--

3] And, it disregards the reason our corporations are sitting on $ 2 trillion in cash--it is folly to think the money will be spent ending unemployment—it also exposes the false claim by the Republicans that cutting taxes for the wealthy will create jobs...and consummate proof of this lie in that THE BUSH TAX CUTS WERE EXTENDED].

4] The market thrives when we have a robust, employed, consuming workforce--and absent that the result is High-Unemployment/Sluggish-Recovery [the current state of both]--

5] Every waking moment in a market economy is spent pondering ways to eliminate as many of us humans, as possible, from the workplace--to increase "profits"--i.e., We should never condemn the CEO for closing a plant when they are losing money--but we should be outraged by a government that is non-responsive to this lapse in the market economy--

HR 870 [currently in Committee] and 15 USC § 3101, specifically address "unemployment" in America--and we have ignored only at our social/economic/political peril--see also, The Neighbor-To-Neighbor Job Creation Act: www.Inclusivism.org

The latter path to ending our unemployment crisis is a Pro-Market "win-win" solution--the American people win, and capitalism wins--

Jim Green

To the editor:

So long as the potential for manipulation of electronic voting continues to exist—our elections in America will be in peril! In spite of all the polls showing a strong Obama victory--it was not until 10PM Central on 11-4-08.....that we could breath a sigh of relief....we had been cheated out of the past two elections....with many believing that Bush was never legally elected president of the United States....and we were braced for the worst.......this can, and MUST be fixed before 2010, so that this never happens again, and in the interest of all who support fair and open elections--regardless of party. Accordingly, it is urged that we adopt the following proposed "FAIL-SAFE ELECTRONIC VOTING ACT":

THE FAIL-SAFE ELECTRONIC VOTING ACT

1) EVERY electronic voting machine (hereafter EVM), must be inexpensive, identical throughout the U.S. in a 1/150 ratio, and *must count and produce a hard-copy of the recorded votes*. In addition, an extra copy of their recorded votes would be produced (not necessarily a hard-copy), marked

"Voter's Copy", and containing "NOTICE: Do Not Destroy Until Every Election On Your Ballot Is Certified". [If Wal-Mart refused to give us a receipt for our purchases—would they not be suspect—and this regards our democracy].

2) *After confirming that their votes are recorded correctly,* the voter would then insert the hard-copy ballot into a software-free (count only) optical scanner (hereafter OS), for a second count. The hard-copy ballot would be retained by election officials in the event a candidate asks for a recount (*not possible under the current system, and*

which undermines the legality of each _such election)._ The EVM and the OS must be manufactured by different companies (which is universally true today).

3) Election officials assigned to oversee the EVM, would be prevented by law from overseeing the OS, and vice-versa, and stiff criminal penalties would be imposed for violations.

4) Further, every EVM would be programmed with raw data re the total registration rolls, by party, and norms for their voting history, etc.,----as an "alert" to a possible irregularity, such as

an "Under-vote"—or "vote-flipping" etc., and _standards_ established to suspend certification where there is an "improbable result", at least temporarily, of a particular election until the discrepancy is cleared up. (This is what computers do best, and it would be very easy to create such a program).

5) At the end of the election day, tallies would be taken from the EVM and the OS, for each candidate. _If the tallies didn't balance for any given election, or if there is an "alert", that election cannot be certified until the "error" is corrected._ If the candidates agree (the victory is certain), minor discrepancies in the

count could be disregarded. While probably rare, the Voter, or a random sample of Voters, would be required by law to return their Copy of the recorded votes to the election office to clear up any "error", or where an "alert" signals the need for same.

6) Further, every state provides for a recount when the total vote falls below a certain percent of difference between the candidates, impossible to conduct with the current EVM—and thus Congress must mandate the following regarding presidential candidates: A RUN-OFF election is mandated and triggered in those states where the

percent of total vote is less than .5% of difference between any given candidates; said election to be held on the second Saturday following the election, on PAPER BALLOTS ONLY, and contain ONLY the names of the relevant candidates, for instance: "Barack Obama, Democrat" and "John McCain, Republican"—with oversight in counting by a representative(s) of each party—said procedure providing more than adequate time to meet the Electoral College mandate. NOTE: Had this been the law in 2000, Al Gore would be our president, and the American economy would not be in meltdown!

7) Finally, absent the above safeguards, and until these safeguards are in place-- Congress must mandate that PAPER BALLOTS, ONLY, can be used in our presidential elections. This is not a "partisan" issue, it is a "pro-democracy" issue. Most importantly, this will return the responsibility for our elections, and our vote counting, back into the hands of the individual voter, where it belongs, and out of the hands of "corporate control"--- *it is after all "our democracy", itself, that is at risk if we don't take these steps---and in that regard, is there any time or cost differential that is too great?*

Jim Green

To the editor [In Closing]:

So where is the Republican apology?
Their profuse apology to the American
people for the insufferable damage they
did to the America people, and
America—since 1981—

Our deficit was a very manageable $60
billion in 1980—and by 2008 the
Republicans had driven our deficit to a
staggering $10 trillion!

So here is the deal: WE, the American
people should demand of Romney [most

likely the Republican nominee—Indeed, to be asked of every Republican in Washington] that they are NOT permitted to say even one more word in this campaign until they profusely apologizes to the American people for the damage Republican policies have done to America since 1980!

Our being patriotic to America demands no less!

Jim Green

ABOUT THE AUTHOR. I was employed in our Criminal Justice System for a cumulative 20 years as a probation officer, with 5 of those years as a chief probation officer. I authored the concept of "Shock Incarceration" which became law in Kansas in 1970, and then was adopted in numerous jurisdictions in the U.S. and also spread to Europe—it is currently identified in the U.S. as "Boot Camp" [as the means to "shock" the young offender—and a total distortion of my original intent—like many ideas, once released, they take on a life of their own]. I was the Democrat candidate for

Congress, District 21, TX, 2000. I would most define myself as a Social Ecologist- - [albeit my degree is in Psychology]. My web page is www.Inclusivism.org – which has been on the internet since 1996.